Aqua

Aqua

Anne Marriott

Wolsak and Wynn . Toronto

Poems in this collection have been published in *ARC*, *B.C.
Books Canadian Literature*, *Canadion Author and Bookman*,
Cormorant, *Matrix*, *The New Quarterly*, *Poetry Canada Review*,
Quarry, *The Writers' Quarterly*, and the anthology *The Dry
Wells of India*.

Typeset in Bookman, printed in Canada by
The Coach House Press, Toronto.

The author wishes to thank the Canada Council for the
encouragement and assistance of a grant to complete this
book. The publishers gratefully acknowledge support by
The Canada Council and The Ontario Arts Council.

Many thanks to Gay Allison and Sharon Nelson for their help
in bringing about the publication of this book.

Wolsak and Wynn Publishers Ltd.
Don Mills Post Office Box 316
Don Mills, Ontario, Canada, M3C 2S7

Canadian Cataloguing in Publication Data
Anne Marriott, 1913-
   Aqua
Poems.
ISBN 0-919897-26-6
I. Title.
PS8526.A77A8 1991   C811'.52   C91-095215-9
PR9199.3.M37A8 1991

Contents

I LIVING UNDER WATER

SUNKEN CITIES

Under all the world's oceans
lie the sunken cities
real or rumoured
differing in catastrophe
as *swept away by a ravening wave*
or *snatched off*
in an earthquake's ravening jaws.
From a few
slink revenants
to warm or torment the land-dwellers.

A few cities were swallowed dry
as *Ephesus, engulfed by soil*
a useful reference now for travellers who
survey its marble streets
then, pulling back the blue
blind surface of the nearby Aegean
with their eyes
construct the same roads, white as bone
add curled columns
a brothel
and a great library where
long seaweed scrawls
are the only message left in rotting books.
Someone adds a palace —
one of Poseidon's lesser residences?

9

And sunken towns are sometimes famed for bells:
any proper English city
fathoms down
has towers and steeples
pealing for Matins and for Evensong
though only fish attend;
or someone illicitly abed
hears the bells clang a portent in his brain
runs homeward
weaving an excuse
There was a mermaid in the estuary!

All the eyes of those who probe
the waves for cities
take on the waters' colours:
cobalt   onyx   jade.
And there's a sunken town in every head
cleverly covered,
only now and then
debris comes up to curdle in the strands
of eyelashes.
Some never take sunglasses off
so no one knows how far the rot has spread.

Watch for the one with something strange
half-hidden by a collar!
There are those who try to live
entirely under water
developing tails and fins,

though always some cell fails to adapt.
They dive further daily.
Suddenly they drown.

Far down, the stony streets
are noiseless.
Skeletons lie
as still as coral
the only movement fish who nose
into green rib-cages.
No hand pulls weedy ropes to swing the bells
yet all around the world a toll
of mourning rises, up
through the surface, starts
the ringed waves running
to the farthest beach.

TO COME TO YOUR SHORE

The only way I can come
to you and to your shore
is by grief
walking over it like a bridge
across the dark inlet
its supports wavering
in the flood tide
or by swimming through the black seas
to your shining island
(but I could never swim).

Grief is like an animal hit by a truck
writhing on the pavement.
Grief is like the thick closing in
of the suffocating tunnel
collapsing in a nightmare.
Grief is a crucifixion
agony
too terrible for any simile.
(But the only way, some say
to a resurrection
to coming to you).

A GRIM TALE

I see it only from
the windows of a train
a place that has no name.

A rocking-horse lies dead.
One rocker's split, legs splayed
to brace against
whatever was the terror that it faced.
The rectangle of sand
rimmed with wood fragments
(once a tidy box)
of course suggests a grave.
A greying paw
uncovered by a twist of wind
shows where a teddy-bear is buried
(there may be others).

The house beyond
stares vacant-windowed
vision skewed by one broken pane.
Was it cursed from the beginning?
— the golden child
cherub, really a changeling?
Monster?

Somewhere in me in darkness something stirs.
I pull down the blind.

LIVING UNDER WATER

First the plunge (escape)
sinking down into the cold
green, surprised perhaps
how cold the green is
and how dark
growing darker as it deepens
almost black
when one gets to the secret sea-bed.
One sees at length
scraped out on a stone
between the barnacles
by some earlier diver
There shall be no light here.

One supposed, of course
that learning to breathe through gills
would be laborious
but not how long the labour lasts.
Then there's the endless itch
as skin corrodes
and thickens into scales.
Never ignore the crabs!
The tiniest still
has pincers
seeking the tender spots
where the new grey skin
hasn't quite closed over.
Even anemones
so flowery, soft
sprout murderous tentacles.

Limpets begin to grow
rooting in one's face like warts.

A flash of phosphorescence
can make it seem worthwhile
for a few minutes, and the quiet
and seclusion (what one came down for)
then one happens
to drift upward
see the shadow of a ship.
Forgotten pictures form
behind watery eyes:
sunlight in cobalt sky
over golden fields, sparkling —
but deadly now. Beached
one could only gasp and shrivel.

This process cannot be reversed.

GRAND TOUR

Tonight's hotel is an old one —
turn-of-the-century.
Dukes of darkest Carinthia
may have slept here
but in the room with the gold-curlicued ceiling
allocated to the rich Americans.
Older
single women
get rooms like themselves: greying.
The wash of centuries came through
leaving sediment in corners.
The beds are still clammy.

From the balcony
with its one, sodden deckchair
I regard a baroque
bulbous church. I feel
I am trying to swallow history
like a whole onion
layer upon layer
Emperors Archdukes Archbishops.
My esophagus strains
around the Lorelei Mayerling
mad King Ludwig
and here Dracula himself
is just over the border.
My gut's crammed with castles.

I get cramps after midnight.
(In all the hotels the toilets flush noisily)
Tomorrow, on to Venice —
bones of Doges
rise in the canals
in the throat.

Two weeks from now, back
in the short familiar sequence
of Canadian history
at great expense I will get
all my pictures developed
arrange them exactly
under plastic in an album —
Europe finally dried out
and under control.

II AQUA

AQUA

i

Water, mysterious
moves underneath the earth
travels its *aquifer*
"a layer of soil
or rock, able to
hold, transmit — "

In dreams we wander
in enormous caves
dripping with stalactites.
grottoes, chambers
some with hidden ponds
open beyond   beyond
limestone shapes change and recede
farther and farther backward
in our minds.

Water above the earth
steams in the sunlight
swells and divides
in glittering skeins
that fall down mountainsides
in beaded curtains.
They tell messages in continuous code
melodious, but hard to understand —
unwarned, heads going under
we are washed into unknown channels.

I have lost sight of water.
Tonight I'm burning for even water's scent
search for a forgotten wand
to go divining
in this shrivelled city where I have to live
(if the wand rises
can I grow green again?).
All I find
is one sickly trickle in a gutter.
Brown silt forms a delta by
the bars that strain the runoff.
Delta. Crop land. The only crop that's here
cigarette-butts, gum-wrappers
a pink inflated breast
ripped from a magazine.
There's a piece of sodden string
someone wound one end of it into a head
left a strand hanging for the venomous tongue.

iii

Love (I pretend
somewhere you can hear this)
we had that stream
once in a rich valley
("We had" but water belongs
to no one but itself).
Remember (you must) up north
looking for a campsite
how we almost missed
the unmarked track
slipping down from the highway.
Something was flowing
shining beyond the trees
which folded back like doors in front of us
so we could see
it seemed for the first time
the whole earth in its valid colours.
Vivid green pulsed from every leaf of grass
blue liquid light
poured from each pine needle in the grove
and beams from the radiant stream
which fed the place
shot silver and golden off its polished banks.

iv

Tonight my lungs
(the last X-Ray
showed the disease advancing)
fill with grey vapours.
The city air
cakes like black pitch inside my nose.

Remember. We made our bed
in the pure night beside the stream.
I went for one more look
at the moonwhite river.
A ripple moved
across its skin and mine —
a watersnake, breaking the crystal?
Cold ran down my arms and thighs
something icy touched my heel.
I ran through the thick grass
to hold your body deep in mine.
Later I told myself
just a peeled branch
rode down the shallows.

v

All of us come in water from the womb —
those three in the cab
passing fast through this noisome street
grandmother, mother, child
the driver in his checkered cap —
no argument.
Debate starts up
whether all of us long
to swim again in that warm, secret pool.
Some of us stand
like children, yet
staring up mouths open
hoping to catch a raindrop
search for moisture sixty years or so
always thirsty.
Perhaps the grave — ? No!
We won't get into that.
Some have, strangely, grown afraid
of that easy element
their aqueous mother.

vi

Remember. The winter
by our tidy southern fire
you talked of settlement
sketched irrigation dams
and sluices (water must be reined
a useful horse).
We would mark the place as ours
by making a garden
(our first mystic parents
lingering in your mind?)

vii

On the shores of sleep each night
we pondered (back in our valley)
where did that sweep of water rise?
It didn't show
on the surveyors' maps you'd ordered.
Once or twice we thought we heard
a tumbling sound
something that rushed and tripped
from a masked crevice.

The puzzle chafed you.

viii

In a dream I hung
high in the black firmament
over the huge north land.
Trees furred it sky to sky
impenetrable
yet all through the country
I could trace the stream
moving, brilliant in the dark.
I strained to see
where it first sprang from
instead
I saw, even from this height
something disturb the flow.
An unnatural eddying.
The snake.

Far below
a voice like mine cried out.
A glassy music echoed from the rocks.

ix

The dry skin of this city night
cracks suddenly. Two blocks away
the jittery pole
of a late tram jumps on its wires.
Light sizzles across the grid
like the stream, grown wayward
splashing the northern sky
with lightning-strokes of green.
It branched, softened
into shoots and leaves
your garden beds transplanted.

One night I saw
the stream had entered in our blood.
Light dripped like water
from our finger-tips.
It never came again.

x

I pace the narrowing room
run the tap a long time
(the water's never cold).
Cool sleep as smooth as cream
soothed us in that valley.
Even so, I began to wake
often, sometimes roused
by the broken sounds of the trapped current.
Clumsy, it lapsed and crumpled
over the ranked logs that made
our private reservoir.

xi

Conflicting tales
confused that final summer.
What happened? Some actually said
that there were floods.
Dams broke
walls of mud and water crashing down
to choke the valleys
changing every course.
Most people claimed
it was the driest year on record
every creekbed dust
everything withered unless
its roots could draw on a far underground supply.
All I know is that I woke
one greyed morning, in the tent —
and you had gone.

We had been making plans
for an expedition upstream.
We would chart every marsh and tributary
until we found at last
that first essential gush of water.
Others had come
through our preserve
and talked of sources —
had you gone with one of them?
Without me?

In the garden
some peculiar blight
had bent and blackened
all the plants.

xii

No moon tonight
to wash the buildings.
Hydro has trouble somewhere —
not a glint of light.
My shrinking shadow is absorbed
into the general darkness.
I can't see the brown runnel
but its odour rises.
I bend and feel the concrete.
It's worn away
like aging bone.
Dust is packed down
in creases in its lumpy hide.

I am so dry
my mouth wrinkles
lips split at the corners.
I'm frightened
what if I lose
the power to swallow?

xiii

Where did you go?
I thought you as clear as water, love
certain as its table underneath the rock.
Did you find the veiled source
of all we'd laid our claim to?
Or did the snake
winding in between the submerged roots
get your ankle with its fangs?
You could have slipped
stepping onto a rock weeds made a trap.
You could have — though you were skilled
in currents —
drowned.

xiv

I know that underneath even
this city, water flows
clear or thickened
through its aquifer of pipes and tunnels.
Culverts crammed with smeary foam
bore their way
under the gritty traffic.
This brownish trickle here
will seep into the main
and join the rest.
But I don't know
where the secret flood begins
nor where's its outfall.

XV

Thalassa. A word I learned
almost before childhood.
Thalassa. The sea.
I know I'd murmur it to myself
cherish it in my mouth
suck on it
for strength and growth.

Thalassa. Is that what rises
now behind my eyes?
Its salt is strong.
Will all snakes finally die?

Wherever that ocean stretches
the earth's soured streams
will sweeten in it.
They merge, braid, broaden
out into the deep.

III   THE ROSE AND THE DAGGER

THE ROSE AND THE DAGGER

Stories from the Island of Rhodes

These poems can be read by a single voice or by the
following:

NARRATOR

THE GUIDE (female)

JOHN (the sad grey man)

WOMAN (his bloated wife)

i

Narrator

The rose
holy flower
round on the ancient coin
lies on the blue water.
Blue. The tourists, world-worn
coming from the jetty
stand dry mouths open
thirsty for such *blue.*
Cliffs pour amber (honey) down
into ultramarine.
Each colour soothes the other.

But the tide turns.
The sea assaults the land
beats on the milky rocks
an infant
wild with hunger
striking before it sucks.

Inland, the tender centre
sweet with the flowers, thyme-scented.
— Suddenly, thunderclap
blood gushes. Pours
down the banks, and pools.

ii

Narrator

Bougainvillaea, the guide explains
holds up her umbrella, magnet.
The tour party clusters.
A sad grey man, named John
his bloated wife
honeymooners from Cologne
English Mum, slim Dad
the kids loud with holiday
Japanese sharp with lenses.

The Guide

I will tell you in English first.
This island full of flowers
is shaped like a dagger! It points
they say at the Turk's heart -- you know
of the Crusades, the knights?
I repeat in German.

Narrator

Crimson flowers
drain out from a dagger-wound in the ribs
of Saracens and stubborn knights
of others stabbed
not always with steel.
Blood runs over all the stones.

42

iii

John

My name is John
one not unconnected with this island
as: Knights Hospitallers
noble intruders
a John their saint and patron.

I am an island
(though another John
declared the opposite).
Buttressed up thick and grey
the slits in my walls
like these built by the knights
are squeezed small, for safety.
Even so an arrow
sometimes finds a mark.

Someone moves beside me
under the gilded walls
someone bloated, circular
trundling on the
cobblestones. She clutches me
cries my name
John John
Who is she?
Why is she here?
How could this ballooning body
swallow the one I loved?
I remember breasts
small like the island's roses.

iv

Narrator

The guide points
up a sheer hill
to a faded temple.

The Guide

Watch your step!

John

There is a sign
the drop is dangerous.
Far below I see the water
knifing into the rocks.
But this woman beside me
cries in fear of falling
holds me
on the first pink step
between the whitewashed houses.

She cannot climb.
I may not.

One night in Crete
I thought I heard a child
crying.
But we had no child.

44

v

Narrator

The great Athena burst
from the skull of Zeus
enlightening the world.
The Athena of this island
remains mysterious
manifestation
poor relation?
Pure virgin born in a cave
sacred now to a later maiden
Mary.

The Guide

Kings brought this Athena gifts
(I will use French in one minute)
That is documented!
On a paving stone
upturned by archaeologists.
It is said she wrought miracles
occasionally.

Narrator

At the foot of the hill
someone is crying
a child's tears.
A child trapped
in a cave
of flesh and fat
walls thick with tallow
a child weeping
frantic to break out.
A child who dreamed long ago
out of a picture book
a headland topped
with rose columns
supporting a burning sky.

Woman

I am trapped in this body
I cannot climb
I thought in this country
some kind of wisdom
would leap into my mind.
There is room for it.
(My father said *There is nothing
in this child's head* said it often).
I stare up. The hot blue
blisters my eyelids.

Narrator

From Athena Lindia's Acropolis
the cliffs run down
brown sugar
crystallized by the waves.
The columns of her broken temples
sticks of stale candy rock
sold at a British seaside.
(Was there an English murmur *peppermint*?)
The cracked stumps of pillars
have been kindly corseted
with chicken wire
by an American foundation
their sign claiming credit.

vi

Narrator

Morning. The sky bleeds
swirls and streaks
the sun, a hot heart
pulses up over the hills
of Asia Minor.
A bay
deep in Athena Lindia's cliffs
begins to glow
by noon the colour tears the eyes.

The Guide

Look over, carefully please!
It is the exact spot
where he landed. The Apostle Paul.

Narrator

Being female, she prefers
John or James or almost any saint
to Paul. Confides to the grey man
that someone in the town
by the Byzantine church
(its walls teem with holy faces, flowers)
reported that a voice
one midnight rose from the bay
Let the women keep silence!

48

Where the turquoise thins out
on the light sand
the apostle stepped ashore.
The chapel marking his footprints
shines, white intensified by blue
alabaster
dazzles
flames.

vii

The Guide

Listen! We come
to the most important tale
in this island's history.
These walls — the Grand Master's palace.
— You all have heard
of course of the Crusades?
The gallant knights?

Narrator

Jerusalem the golden
with blood and booty blest
beneath thy contemplation
the battle cannot rest —
swords of knights and Saracens
slashed sweaty air
shoulders and bellies.
The pale sand burst
into bloom. A vast carpet
embroidered with roses.

The Guide

The Knights Hospitallers retreated to Acre.

50

Narrator

The tourists listen
blank in the tired afternoon
all but the fat woman
toiling always
an archway behind.

The Guide

Then they fled!
(They could not believe
the cursed unbelievers were victors.)
They came to this island
warned of this goddess here
though she was a pure virgin.
Now, this is part
of the authentic fortress!
Alas, healers became harriers —

Narrator

The guide has a degree
from a fine university,
is proud of her vocabulary.
The grey man's face
is a stone.

The Grand Master awaited
the pillage in his palace
feet measuring out
black and white pebbles
of patient mosaic.
A knight with skin
not yet harsh from the wind
hair tender as a girl's
waited under the pointed
shadow of a cypress.
Someone came into port,
came in the entrance
where Colossus once fell.

The Guide

It took nine hundred
and eighty camels
to carry off his fragments!

Narrator

Someone lands, strides
determined
up the long narrow
Street of the Knights.

52

viii

The Woman

Where has he gone?
He has left me to stumble
my feet turn over
on these dusty stones.

For an hour I have stood
outside the apothecary's
(the guide saw me, called
but I made no movement)
Where has he gone?
My body is stiff
with the fear of falling.
How could I rise?

In the window beside me
I escape into childhood.
Supplies for infants
hungry infants, crying
beating their fists.
My mouth is a cave
dark and dry. I draw
the nipple smoothly
into my mind
delicious smoothness.
My tongue slides over and over it.
I gulp sweet saliva.
Where has he gone?

ix

Narrator

Everyone came here
staining the perfumed island
with each other's blood.
Everyone comes here:
the guide's mouth
is sour as she listens
to the languages
regards the summer roads
overripe with tourists
the long pods of alleys
swollen soon to burst
with round moist faces.

The Guide

Everyone came here.
Phoenicians Venetians
Byzantines Genoese
modern Italians —
notice these restorations!
We call them Mussolini Gothic!
I have mentioned knights and Turks —
how many knights
withstood how many Turks?
Ten thousand two hundred thousand?
In the end a traitor knight
breached the great fortress.
(One can only be defeated from inside.)

Narrator

The infidels poured in the gap
like boiling oil.

But the Turkish cemetery is cool
sleeps, quiescent.
Silence lies heavy
as a patterned tile
blue from a mosque
weighing on the hand.
Tombstones are made in different shapes
for men and women
but all stones tilt the same
settling in the soil.
The inscriptions —
unknown names
in a strange alphabet —
wear away under centuries
of Aegean wind.

X

The Guide

One of the party is missing!

Narrator

The guide, agitated, recounts heads.
(Did she fall
or was she pushed? — always
the classic question)
The larger question here
how could she have climbed?
— the body too broken to tell
if she had dragged her monstrous self
on her vast knees
up the path until it ran with red.
The donkey men knew nothing
caring only for their animals
(their investment).
Besides — how
could she have mounted?

Athena Lindia
worked none of her reputed miracles
for this pilgrim,
nor Paul
yearning to be out
of the vexed body himself.

Did the child
imprisoned inside her, suffocating
all at once stab her
shove from within
in all directions
topple her from the cliff
breaking out
floating free?

There are dark petals scattered down the cliff.
Far below
the brilliant sea laps at the golden rocks
licking the blood and body.

The metal stags
guarding the harbour mouth
are silent in the night.
In the palace a dying bug
lies on the mosaic floor
soft black pebble.
In the museum courtyard
the Venetian lion stands
rigid even at rest,
his eyes gouged out.
His mane erodes with time.
The guide turns in sleep.
Tomorrow, on to Mykonos.

Faint mist, almost invisible
forms and reforms
reshapes
wraiths on the cooling rocks.
By daybreak mists are gone
fresh roses, voracious, open.
The first tourist steps ashore from a new ship.
Smiling in the brightening blue
the island waits.

IV   DEATH IN THE CARIBOO

DEATH IN THE CARIBOO

i   Cemetery

High summer: dry silk air
the curved country fields
smell like biscuits.
I have brought my son here.
I am searching for peace.
I have disconnected the radio.

The grasses shine;
the line of woodland glitters.
A good place for lunch!
(he is hungry).
I suggest *under this pine* —
but the glitter draws him,
not a known light on leaves and branches
but an alien gleam
irresistible.

Broken vines sprout,
try to make a cover
hand-over-hand
up cracked headlamps, windshields,
erupting wheels, bumpers.
The simple thicket is complex
with rods and axles.

But the glitter still entices us
a new bright body
squashed like a sardine-can
(the chipmunks can have our sandwiches)
a van —
Don't get into it!
but he does anyway
You can still see the blood!
Something's in his hand
a miniature van   toy
like a dead embryo
something brown on its fender.

The sweet gold country
breathes around us
softly
stretching and living.
My son says
Think of dying
so small

ii   An actual instance

C.M. Blessing   1862
gruesome murder
the sign informs the tourists.
The grave itself is further in,
solitary
in the frayed edge of the forest.
Gruesome
We think dismemberment at least
pieces of limbs
turning up all over the country
among the stones and sand
tossed by the miners,
a nugget embedded
in rotting fingers.
But reading on
shot in the back of the head
gruesome enough   of course
for the occupant,
and, another traveller tells us,
for the discoverer —
a shot in the back of the head
going in neatly (he says)
coming out
to spatter the face in all directions,
flecks of teeth
sprinkling like gold dust
among the pine needles on the sand.

iii   Battle Bluff

It hangs
over the campsite
in the sunset
colour of old blood.

From the top the chief
(his name differs
with the location
Battle Bluffs being found
all over the continent)
— the mighty chief
threw off his enemies one by one
as lightly as my son
tosses Saskatoon berries.
The meadow below ran dark.

Shadows twist in the air currents —
cartwheeling bodies;
shriek, breaking thud —
a predator guts a mouse,
a stone falls into dry berry bushes.

Quick, find firewood
whatever will burn.
The blackness closes.
The moon's light is undependable.

The river is circling,
stalking us.
Fetching
water I see a gleam
in the mudbank
something white   eroded.
How long does an old bone last?

IN THIS RIVER VALLEY

You're *watching for a letter*
but what is there to write?
That each evening wind rises
in this river valley?
Trees fret and rattle,
rush toward the canyon —
some have actually been uprooted.
If I take my hand from this paper
it will blow
down the striated wall
be drowned in the current.

Watching for a letter
but what can I tell you
that you do not know?
The hills across the river
will soon lose their detail
like a face in memory,
become only cutouts
on the golden sky.
Yet wind stirs nerves
feelings, like the pine-needles
so I rush toward you
without moving from this rock.

If you watch for a letter
all you will receive
is an old post-card
wish you were here.
looking over the river's
dimming pattern
longing to lift like ospreys
one fierce joyous swoop
free together
up   over   into
that glowing world.

In this river valley
the light each evening
leaves me now earlier.
Already it's almost too dark to write.
Night fills the valley
I tell you *slowly.*
But with darkness
suddenly
all the wind stops.

CRYING IN SLEEP

The old dog cries out in sleep
his blind head pressed
against my ankle.
I run my hand for comfort
down his thinning fur
frail skin
the brittle bones
that feel like broken shells
washed up on that far-off beach
where once he ran and barked
at threatening waves.
Don't let him die tonight!
The ground is frozen hard.
I could not bury him
in his own place.

I cried in sleep last night
dreaming I waded in
the shallows on that beach.
Undertow   snatched me   tightened
swept me out.
Drowning I fought for breath,
screaming
I woke.
The old dog licked my cheek.

CONCERT IN THE ANTHROPOLOGICAL MUSEUM

Darkness seeps over
into us
blackest green
of an Emily Carr painting
but with no life in it.
The totems stand
hulking students in a school
for primitive delinquents
regimented now, hygienic.

Woodwinds begin a dirge.
Cold, atonal
it inscribes on the dim air
dead shells of huge sea-beasts
giant chrysalises
in a monstrous collector's
cabinet. I sit
beside a wild wooden creature
tamed unto death.
The clarinet weeps.

Is there a shaman's pipe?
Steal in here at midnight
(miraculously subduing
the alarm)
lead them out
of this scientifically controlled

protracted dissolution
back to their Haida forest.
At least let them sink into
living humus.

As for now
before the attendants
can muster to quell
the least creak of rebellion
make these silent ones
know
where they belong —
let's have some drums!

V REGARDING DEATH

INVADER

So, you've arrived.
Your black forepaw
covered with thorny hair
nudges my pale arm.
Master of metamorphosis you change
separate yourself in fragments
specks that move, a column
of black pincered ants
along my veins, glands, bones.
I'm surprised the scan shows nothing of them
though the place where you broke in
is clearly scarred.

Nothing is truly mine now.
Can I bend
mind and muscle where I wish
or will your force from the opposing side
push harder?

I'll work to learn your stifling ways
outwit you any way I can.
Of course you'll be the winner in the end
but at least while I've got sight
I'll meet you eye to eye
eyeball to eyeball
until my final breath I'll stare you out!

RETROSPECTIVE

Where did the train start?
All our eyes
were blind with blood and sleep.
For miles a low mist covered the ground.
We think we travel northward
speculate: *is there an engineer?*
No one has seen him.

Odd things lie beside the track —
clues to locality?
There was a doll
eyeless in gravel
a fishing-rod left spearing
a wide stream, prune-coloured
just now a store, steps worn
wood hammered on
to cover its cracked windows.

Late afternoon now. Some passengers begin
to take down coats and bags
their final station imminent?
Outside a blade of sun
cuts out a single aspen.
It confirms our season —
all the leaves still gold
all of them tinged with grey.

SHEOL

I learned of it from those
old Hebrew psalmists —
David, Asaph, unnamed singers
standing on the crumbling rim
crying out
let me not go down!
Grey winds echoed through
the shapeless spaces
under them.
Light faded slowly.

Some of their neighbours (so I read)
held that their heroes
princes, too
might go to some golden country
sent their opulent jewelry with them
just in case.
Common people
nothing before them but
the crawling leprous shades
tried to hang on —
bad as it was —
here.

EXIT

(The natural earth
scares us with metaphors
we pave them out of sight
inventing more
more obvious)

Never clearly marked
it differs with the maps
fingering off from the highway suddenly.
A driver ahead is drawn away
before he has time to signal
is out of sight in seconds.
We speculate as to where he may have gone
the possible nature of the territory.

More uncertain signs are coming up.
We switch lanes quickly
putting more space between
us and an undesired turnoff
making a barrier
if only of air.

We have a long way
(we believe)
to go yet.

DEATH WISHES

Never build under a volcano!
I was warned early
shown actual photographs
places once lived in utterly trodden down
by prehistoric beasts.
Clearly I heard beams snapping
the hopeless cries
of those caught by the fiery lava herd.

From a train I take often
looking across a canyon
praised by tourists for its depth
their fear
I see split-levels, perfectly landscaped
on the edge.
Our cars thumping start
a small tremor — a few stones fall
across the chasm.
There's a trickle of sand.

From the tiered gardens no one sees
the crooked cave-mouth
how it burrows in darker, deeper,
underneath the barbecues, the swings.

IMITATIONS

Sleep wears the closest likeness.
In my twelfth summer
I lay awake all night
hearing, faint from downtown
screech of a car
siren on a street
that crimsoned in my mind.
Towards morning there was a harsh bird.
I lay awake —
fighting off sleep, in terror.
What if I never woke?
At last the doctor gave me pills.
I struggled in tangled shadows all night long.
In daylight, reading poems
I saw the mythical river, oblivion-pale,
cried out with Keats *go not to Lethe!*

Just last year
I stood in his room in Rome
looked down from his window
at the careless square.
In the coughing traffic
heard his bloody throes
the real
red dying.

DEATH OF A LOVER

Don't touch me
All your hands (my friends)
curl back
like tortoise-heads
into their patterned shells.
Your caring words
shrink into your mouths' centres —
sea-anemones.
I should have tried
to make you understand
the only touch I'd bear
would be soft chestnut fingers
firm palms of the oak.
But not green leaves!
Not even amber.
Those I want heaped on me are wet and brown
as damp and dark
as a certain grave
on a pouring afternoon
leaves
silently
covering death over.

AFTER A MEETING OF POETS

Everyone's gone.
Rooms gape
huge melancholy yawns.
Everyone's gone
from lobbies, corridors
but not from in my head;
a noisy frieze
you faces, eyes
are clearer than these walls
and doors
indelibly inscribed.

Going homeward
all your planes can crash
yet you'll still smile and scowl
make motions, argue
each face outlined with light
inside my restless skull.

My forebears all
ripened into long old age
so predictions are quite good
I'll keep you going for years
my sharpest memory marked *reserved*
your names heaped on my tongue.

For myself? All that I ask
is that when I have to leave
there'll be a survivor
with a space for me
talking and scribbling in his brain
insisting he recall
my life's essential act:
I wrote poems
as
did all of
you.

THE FACTS OF --

My aunt the artist
kept a ham for days
in her dim warm pantry.
Peering in
for biscuits I could not believe
I saw the meat's edge move.

But asleep that night I searched
again for my black cat
missing a week (or weeks?)
Hit and run
hurled under the hedge
its polished fur looked pale
and mottled, ruffling —
Go in the house! my father said.

Riding sweet grass pastures
my horse shied.
I saw, up close
a sheep's seething carcase.
Kicked up my horse but even as he raced
knew however long my life
never could I outrun
the sight
the fact.

I screamed over the fields
a simple sentence
pressed it, branded it
on the wind
please burn me.

THE LAKE

My mother went in first
her thin white hair
a mist on the dull water.
My husband floated on his back
as he used to swim
but made no motions.
The water opened for him
like an envelope.

My father dived in boldly
certain there was an outlet.
My dog swam with all his strength
gave out suddenly
a wave filling his blind eyes.

And all the others — my first
music teacher
her stiff back turning sodden
my uncle
determined to avoid
the queen's telegram of congratulation
my dear friend
trying to see northward to the very end
where *frozen fire* burns over lakes of ice.

This lake is muddied.
At the shallow end
thick pale weeds wait
to snake out
pull me down with the others.

I keep well back
but this dark morning see
all at once around the edge
the water's rising.

THE CURTAIN

As I lay dying
it closed in
familiar, known
in a thousand nightmares
blanket cloth or plush. Dark brown.
I tried to push it
off my face
hands growing numb
my hair sopping with sweat.

After a long time
a nurse said *open
up your eyes
it's morning
you have made it.*
The pale light was clear
the air
smelling of disinfectant, vomit
sweet as a coastal spring
over my mouth.
I gulped it like fresh water.

The question stays
the only one that seems worth asking now
*did I
did I not*
see past that stifling fearful edge
the finest line of brightness?

THE CIRCULAR VILLAGE

Now that daily I spend time
regarding death
I think of you more and more
dear T.S.; my own
enlightenment when I first heard you
your round village.
For fifty years I've searched for it
East Coker
ancestral, Christian
once was even in
the very next county
but no one would come
to guide me to the border.

I've seen its trees, all cut
into perfect circles.
I know its roads
are crescents, melding at their ends
into completeness
promises and hopes
in my beginning
in my end
my beginning.

Brilliant over its roofs
a pulsing comet
swallows its own tail
spins just above treetops.
Leaves heat and quiver
glowing
one here and there will blaze
none ever burn.

Welsh Henry saw it
over the farther boundary
three hundred years before us
ring of endless light.

A Note about the Author

Born and educated in Victoria, British Columbia, Anne
Marriott has published nine books of poetry, the second
of which, *Calling Adventurers*, won the 1941 Governor
General's Award for poetry. Her publications include
The Wind our Enemy (1939), *Sandstone and Other Poems*
(1945), *Countries* (1971), *The Circular Coast* (1981), and
Letters from Some Islands (1986). She lives in
Vancouver, British Columbia.